American Humane.

*Protecting
Children & Animals
Since 1877*

American Humane Pet Care Library

Dogs

How
to
Choose
and
Care
for
a Dog

Laura S. Jeffrey

Enslow Publishers, Inc.

40 Industrial Road	PO Box 38
Box 398	Aldershot
Berkeley Heights, NJ 07922	Hants GU12 6BP
USA	UK

http://www.enslow.com

American Humane®

Protecting
Children & Animals
Since 1877

The American Humane Association is dedicated to preventing the cruelty, abuse, neglect, and exploitation of children and animals. To learn how you can support the vision of a nation where no child or animal will ever be a victim of willful abuse or neglect, visit www.americanhumane.org, phone (303) 792-9900, or write American Humane at 63 Inverness Drive East, Englewood, Colorado, 80112-5117.

Library of Congress Cataloging-in-Publication Data

Jeffrey, Laura S.
    Dogs: how to choose and care for a dog / Laura S. Jeffrey
       p. cm. — (American humane pet care library)
    Summary: Explains who to consult, where to go to pick the right dog,
       and how to keep them happy and healthy.
    Includes bibliographical references and index.
    ISBN 0-7660-2520-9
    1. Dogs—Juvenile literature. [1. Dogs. 2. Pets.] I. Title.
    SF426.5.J456 2004
    636.7—dc22

                            2003022971

Printed in the United States of America

10 9 8 7 6 5 4

Contents

Many
people
enjoy the
company
of dogs.

1
A Best Friend

Dogs are great pets. They give their owners a lot of love and devotion. All they ask for in return is care and attention. Dogs can also be active and eager buddies. You can take long walks and runs with them. It is no wonder that dogs are known as "man's best friend." Millions of Americans are dog owners.

This book will help you choose the right dog for you. It will tell you what to feed your new pet and why you should train your dog. It will tell you how to make your new pet feel comfortable and safe. You will learn how to keep your dog healthy and happy.

You can play ball with your dog and teach it to fetch a Frisbee.

There are
many
different
breeds
of dogs.

2

The History of Dogs

 Dogs have been household pets for thousands of years. Long, long ago, however, dogs were wild animals.

Pictures of dogs have been found on cave walls. Pictures have also been found in tombs from Europe and the Middle East.

The ancient Egyptians thought of dogs as gods. Some dogs had their own servants and their own gold. They were fed the finest foods. Many Egyptian rulers were buried with their

Dogs and people learned to live with each other more than 14,000 years ago. Pictures of dogs have been found on walls in ancient tombs in Egypt.

favorite dog. The rulers believed that their dog would protect them in an afterlife.

People started breeding dogs for the different types of work they could do. Dogs were used to guard and protect people and property. Other kinds of dogs were used on farms to herd animals. Dogs were used to hunt, too.

Today, there are millions of dogs in the world. Most of them are owned as pets. There are about four hundred different breeds of dogs. Dogs can also be mixtures of different breeds.

The Saint Bernard is one type of breed. Monks in the Swiss Alps were the first to

Saint Bernards can be trained to help find people that may be lost in the snow.

Guide dogs are very important. They help blind and visually impaired people get around by themselves. Guide dogs have to be trained in a special way. This dog is learning how to lead the man onto the bus.

---

use Saint Bernard dogs. These big dogs guided people along snow-covered paths. Saint Bernards were also trained to help rescue travelers. With their good sense of smell, they were able to find people trapped deep in the snow. The dogs were trained to lie down on the people to keep them warm and to bark until help arrived.

The German Shepherd is another type of dog breed. The German army used them as military dogs during World War I. Soldiers from the United States and England brought these dogs home with them after the war. They are often used as guard dogs. They are used by the police as well as search-and-rescue teams. They are one of the breeds of dogs that are trained as guide dogs for the blind. They can also be trained as service dogs for people with disabilities.

Dogs can live for sixteen years, or more, depending on their breed and health. With proper care, they will give their owners love and friendship for many years.

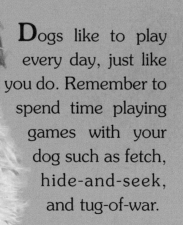

Pet Pointer

Dogs like to play every day, just like you do. Remember to spend time playing games with your dog such as fetch, hide-and-seek, and tug-of-war.

3

The Right Dog for You

 What type of dog is best for you? Selecting the right animal is the key to a long and happy relationship. First, you should decide if you want a dog or a puppy. Puppies are cute, but they are like babies. They need a lot of attention. In fact, they need more care and training than a grown dog does. A puppy also has plenty of energy. A puppy will need play time with you. It will also need toys to keep it busy when you cannot play.

Puppies need a lot of attention.

You and your family can decide which dog is right.

Another decision is what breed of dog to get. Some dogs are better for children and families. You can learn about the different breeds of dogs through the Internet or library books, or from the staff at an animal shelter.

Animal shelters and animal welfare groups can help match the right dog to the right people.

Where Will You Get Your New Pet?

Your first stop should be the local animal shelter or an animal welfare group. There you will find cute and loving puppies and dogs in need of a home.

The people who care for animals at the shelter have gotten to know them. They will help match you with the right pet for your family.

If you want a certain breed that is not currently available at the shelter, ask shelter workers about good ways to find that breed.

Some communities have breed-placement groups. These are groups of concerned people who take in unwanted dogs, usually of one breed they like, and find homes for them. There are also resources for finding sheltered purebred dogs on the Internet.

You can also buy a dog or puppy directly from a breeder. However, you will probably spend more to get a pet from a breeder than from a shelter. Responsible breeders have clean facilities. They do not let their dogs have puppies too often. They keep the dogs' living space clean and play with them. Good breeders are sometimes selective about who buys their puppies.

You can find many different dogs at the animal shelter or a local animal welfare group.

The American Humane Association says people should not get a dog from a pet store. Pet stores are not as concerned about matching people with a pet that will fit well into their lifestyle. Also, most pet stores buy puppies from different breeders. Many of those breeders do not take good care of their animals. They may breed them too often, keep them in crowded or dirty housing, or treat the dogs poorly. This type of situation is known as a "puppy mill."

Pet Pointer

Whenever your dog is outside of your yard, it should wear a leash. If your dog is on a leash, it cannot run into the street and get hit by a car or get lost.

You are going to be excited when
you bring home your new dog.

4

Taking Care of Your Dog

You probably cannot wait to spend time playing with your new pet. But you need to give it time to get to know its new home. When you first bring your dog home, you may want to keep it in one room or a crate. Take several days to let the dog get to know each room of the house. The dog will feel more secure if it learns its way at its own pace. If you need information on crate training, talk to your veterinarian or workers at the animal shelter.

Give your new dog time to get to know you.

Pet Pointer

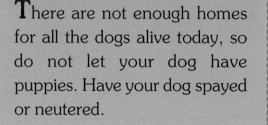

There are not enough homes for all the dogs alive today, so do not let your dog have puppies. Have your dog spayed or neutered.

Crate training, when done properly, can help a dog feel safe and secure. But dogs should not live in crates all the time.

If you are bringing a puppy home, make sure your home is "puppy proof." Puppies are active and curious. A puppy will sniff, play with, or chew almost anything in its reach. Safely put away trash cans, electrical cords, dangerous chemicals and cleaners, loose change, and medicine. Make your house a safe one for your new friend.

Make sure your dog always has water available.

Feeding

Always have a bowl of fresh, cool drinking water for your dog. Feed your dog a high-quality, brand-name food made just for it. Puppies need food made just for puppies. After a year, most dogs can eat adult formula. Some large breeds of dogs need to eat puppy food until they are a few months older. Your veterinarian can help you figure out if your dog has special eating needs.

Choose foods labeled "complete," "balanced," or "fully nourishing." By law these words mean that your dog will be getting all it needs for its diet.

Puppies need three or four meals a day until they are three months old. At six months old, puppies can be fed twice a day. By the time your dog is over one year old, you can feed him once a day. Some dogs can be fed twice a day. Check with your vet.

To figure out how much dog food to feed your dog, read the food label.

To figure out how much food to give your dog, read the food label. The amount your pet needs is based on the dog's weight. Also keep in mind your dog's age and activity level. Do not overfeed your dog. More and more dogs are becoming obese because their owners are giving them too much food. Give your pet fifteen to twenty minutes to finish its meal, and then take away the feeding dish. If any food remains, give your dog slightly less at the next meal.

Sleeping

Your dog will need a warm, comfortable place to relax and sleep. The best place for a dog to sleep is in a house, in either its own doggie bed or in a crate. If you use a crate, learn special ways to train your dog with the crate.

Fast Fact

Dogs can live to be over ten years old. Before you adopt one, make sure you can care for your pet for its entire life.

If your dog sleeps outside, make sure it has shelter from the heat and cold. Also, make sure the dog's house is the right size for it. A house that is too big will not keep a dog warm. Keep the house clean and dry. If the weather is extremely hot or extremely cold, bring your dog inside.

Housebreaking

If you bring a puppy home, you will need to "housebreak" it. That means teaching it to eliminate, or "go to the bathroom," outside the house. A puppy will not know where to eliminate unless you train it. This takes time and patience. Just like a person, your puppy will make mistakes. A puppy needs to learn how to control its bladder and bowels.

Scolding or punishing your dog will not help with housebreaking. In fact, it may make housebreaking harder. Be prepared to let your new puppy outside every few hours. Be sure to say good things each time it does a good job. Remember that the most important times to let your dog out are right after it wakes up and right after it eats.

New puppies need to be housebroken. Patience and praising will help your puppy understand when and where it should go to eliminate.

Some adult dogs need housebreaking. But once they know the word "out" and where it takes them, there should be no problem with accidents. If an accident does occur, make sure to clean the spot well with a product that removes pet stains and odors. That way, the dog will not pick that spot again.

Identification

Every year, thousands of pets are turned in to animal shelters because they do not have proper identification. One of the easiest and least expensive ways to protect your pet is by placing an identification tag on its collar. The tag should have your family's name, address, and phone number on it. Also, ask the adults you live with to find out if you need a city or county license for your dog.

Your dog should have a collar and an ID tag. If your dog ever gets lost, the tag will help the person who finds your pet find you.

A microchip is a very small computer chip. More and more people are having vets put microchip IDs into their dogs. This is a safe way to have a permanent ID for your dog. But some people who find dogs are unaware that they may have a microchip. So it is a good idea to have an identification tag on your pet's collar at all times. That way, you are helping your pet find its way home if it ever becomes lost.

Fast Fact

Did you know that the dog family includes wolves, coyotes, and foxes?

Keeping your dog healthy takes time and attention.

5

Healthy and Happy

A vet makes sure animals stay healthy. Keeping your dog healthy takes time and attention. Adult dogs should visit the vet at least once a year for an annual exam and any needed vaccine boosters. Puppies need additional visits for vaccinations.

A veterinarian, often called a vet, is a doctor who takes care of sick and hurt animals.

27

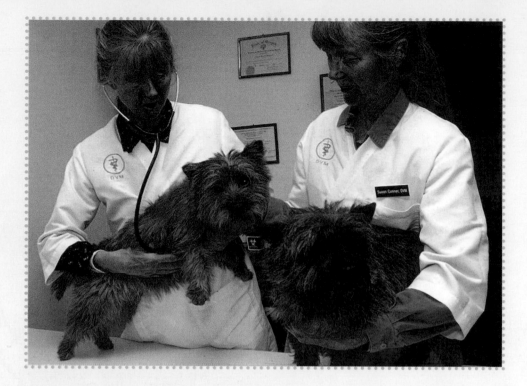

Bring your dog to the vet every year. Some puppies may need to go more than once a year.

Spaying and Neutering

The vet will want to talk to you and the adults you live with about getting your dog spayed, if it is a female, or neutered, if it is a male. To spay or neuter is to operate on an animal so it cannot reproduce. Spaying and neutering stops overpopulation.

Every year, millions of lovable dogs and puppies must be euthanized, or put to death, in animal shelters because there are no homes available for them. Most animals in local shelters are spayed or neutered before they are put up for adoption.

Spaying and neutering are safe operations. Also, the operation is helpful to your dog. Spayed and neutered pets make better family members. They are less likely to be aggressive or roam. They usually are calmer and loving. Dogs can be spayed or neutered as early as six to eight weeks old.

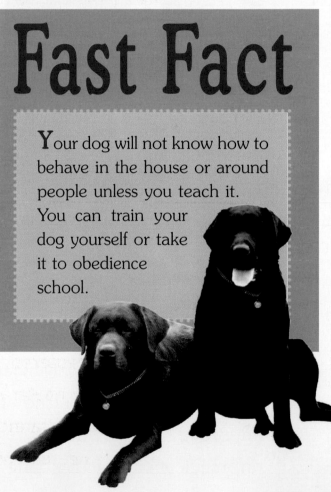

Fast Fact

Your dog will not know how to behave in the house or around people unless you teach it. You can train your dog yourself or take it to obedience school.

Grooming

To keep your pet healthy and looking good, you will need to groom it. Longhaired dogs should be groomed daily so that their fur will not mat or get things stuck in it.

Even shorthaired dogs should be groomed at least once a week to remove loose hair and keep their coat healthy.

Grooming is also a good way to find pests such as fleas, ticks, lice, and mites. These parasites can cause serious diseases and skin problems. Many products are available to help control pests. Talk with your vet before buying anything. This is especially important if your dog is very young, very old, is on medication, or has any other health problems.

Grooming keeps your dog looking healthy.

The vet can recommend the right kind of pest-control powder or spray for your pet. Be sure to read the directions carefully before you put the product on your pet.

Pay attention to your dog's nails and teeth. Be sure to keep your dog's nails trimmed. Long nails can make it hard for a dog to get around. A veterinarian or professional dog groomer can trim your dog's nails. Or, you can buy clippers at your local pet store and do it yourself.

Cleaning your dog's teeth is also important. Bad teeth and gum disease can affect your

dog's health. You should brush your dog's teeth regularly. Also, give it chew toys. The vet will check your dog's teeth during its annual exam. The vet can also show you the best technique for brushing your dog's teeth.

Exercising

Dogs also need regular exercise. A fenced yard is a great place for your dog to play. But do not let this become

its only outdoor activity. Walking your dog at least once a day gives you some special time with your pet. It also gives your pet great exercise that it cannot get in a fenced yard. A daily walk lets your pet make friends with other dogs in the neighborhood. Buy your dog a leash, and plan on taking it

Taking your dog for a walk is a great way for your dog to get exercise and meet other dogs.

for regular walks. (Make sure to take plastic bags and a "pooper scooper" to clean up after your dog. It is the neighborly thing to do and the law in many communities.)

33

Training is
very important
for your dog.
You can teach
your dog to sit.

6

Preventing Problems

Training

A playful and active puppy can be cute, but an untrained adult dog is annoying. For this reason, as well as your pet's safety, you should train your dog. It should be taught to come when its name is called. It should learn to sit and stay and to heel on a leash. Your dog should also learn to obey the "down" command.

Training gives dogs a chance to use their brain and makes them a better pet. Training also

Dogs like to be trained.

35

helps your dog learn that you are in charge. This makes playing with your dog easier.

A great way to learn how to train your dog is by going to a dog obedience class with your pet. There are also books and videos on training dogs. Or, you can take your dog to a professional trainer.

If you decide to train your dog yourself, you will need to set aside ten to twenty minutes every day to work on training.

You can teach your dog to shake your hand.

Make sure these training sessions are in a quiet place with nothing around to distract the dog. Be sure to always use the same commands. Praise your dog for a job well done. Good words and rewards will help your dog become a good friend.

Pet Pointer

Always make sure your dog is wearing an identification tag with your family's name, address, and phone number on it.

Even trained dogs can run into problems if they are allowed to roam. Roaming dogs can get hit by cars, or they can become lost. They can get into fights with other animals or be hurt by bad people who go after loose animals. They can get ill from eating trash or poisonous chemicals or from coming into contact with diseases carried by other dogs. To keep your dog safe, do not let it roam. Keep it in your house or outside in a fenced yard. When your pet wants to go out, walk it on a leash.

Separation Anxiety

Some dogs experience "separation anxiety." This means they get upset when someone they care about leaves the house. Dogs who have separation anxiety bark a lot when they are left alone. They may also destroy things or eliminate in the house.

Some dogs get upset if you leave them alone for long periods of time.

Having problems training your dog? Ask your vet or a worker at a local animal shelter or animal welfare group to help you.

If your dog has separation anxiety, you should not punish it. Dogs have a very short memory, so they will not understand why they are being punished. When you get angry over a mess your dog created hours ago, your pet will not link your anger with the mess.

Instead of punishing your pet, work to change its behavior. For example, dogs pick up on clues that you are leaving. They hear you pick up your backpack. They see you put on your coat and head for the door. They get upset even before you go. You can help your dog by not putting on a big display of affection before you leave or when you arrive home.

You should also practice leaving. Pick up your backpack and put on your coat. But instead of walking out the door, sit on the couch for a few minutes. Then put your backpack and coat away. Do this every day until your dog gets used to it.

Then, begin leaving your dog for short periods of time. Make your first time leaving very short, only five or ten minutes. When you come back, greet your dog, but do not make your greeting too happy. If your dog shows any signs of anxiety during these brief times, make your time away even shorter. Once your dog proves it can be left alone for ten minutes, you can try leaving for up to thirty minutes. This training will teach your dog not to be upset whenever you leave.

Do not worry if your pet suddenly has behavior problems. It is not uncommon for this to happen. Just remember that most problems can be solved. A veterinarian or people at the local humane society can help you.

Be patient with your dog.

41

You and your
dog will be
happy for
many years.

7

A Friend for Life

After you bring a dog into your home, you will be happy to spend time with it there. But there is even more you can do. You can take it to parks near your home and even on vacation.

Remember that dogs can live to be more than ten years old. Keep loving and learning more about your pet, and you and your dog will spend many happy years together.

To adopt a pet, or to help out, contact a local animal welfare group.

Life Cycle

2. By the time it is one year old, a puppy is almost fully grown. By now, it is no longer a puppy, but a dog.

1. A puppy's eyes are closed at birth. They open after a few weeks.

# of a Dog

3. Small- and medium-sized dogs can live for about sixteen years. Large dogs live about ten years.

Words to Know

breed—To control when an animal reproduces; a group of animals with similar features.

housebreak—To teach an animal how to live inside a house and eliminate, or "go to the bathroom," outdoors.

microchip—A very small computer chip put inside an animal as an identification tag.

mixed breed—Having features from more than one breed of animal.

neuter—To perform an operation so a male animal cannot reproduce.

purebred—Belonging to a breed with the same features through many generations of animals.

spay—To perform an operation so a female animal cannot reproduce.

veterinarian—A doctor who takes care of animals.

Learn More About Dogs

Books

Berman, Ruth. *My Pet Dog*. Minneapolis, Minn.: Lerner Publications, Co., 2001.

Evans, Mark. *Puppy*. New York: Dorling Kindersley, 1992.

O'Neill, Amanda. *Dogs*. New York: Kingfisher, 1999.

Petersen-Fleming, Judy, and Bill Fleming. *Puppy Care and Critters, Too!* New York: Tambourine Books, 1994.

Internet Addresses

How to Love Your Dog: A Kid's Guide to Dog Care
<http://www.kidsanddogs.bravepages.com>
This site has more information about dogs.

Just For Kids: Dogs
<http://www.americanhumane.org/kids/dogs.htm>
Learn more about dogs from this site by the American Humane Association.

Index

A

American Humane
    Association, 15
animal shelter, 13, 14,
    17, 24, 29, 39
animal welfare group,
    13, 14, 39, 43

B

breed, 6, 8, 9, 10, 13,
    14, 19
breeders, 14–15
breed placement groups,
    14

C

crate training, 17, 18, 21

D

doggie bed, 21

E

euthanized, 29

F

feeding, 19
    food, 19, 20, 21
    water, 19

G

German Shepherd, 9–10
grooming, 30–32

bathing, 31
gum disease, 31
nail trimming, 31
pest control, 30, 31
teeth cleaning, 31–32
guard, 8, 10
guide dogs, 9, 10

H

house, 17, 21–22
housebreaking, 22–23
    accidents, 23

I

identification, 24–25
    identification tag, 24,
        37
    license, 24
    microchip, 25

N

neutering, 18, 28, 29

O

obedience school, 29,
    36
overpopulation, 28

P

pet store, 15
play time, 10, 11
police dogs, 10

"pooper scooper," 33
puppy mill, 15
"puppy proofing," 18
purebred, 14

R

rescue, 9, 10

S

Saint Bernard, 8–9
sense of smell, 9
separation anxiety,
    38–41
service dogs, 10
sleeping, 21
spaying, 18, 28, 29

T

training, 35–38, 39
    "down" command, 35
    praise, 23, 37
    reward, 37

V

vaccination, 27
vaccine booster, 27
veterinarian, 17, 19, 20,
    25, 27, 28, 30, 31,
    32, 39, 41

W

walking, 32, 33